AF521666

THE NOAH AND NOEL SERIES:
ADVENTURES AND TOYS

By: Nancy K. Carty
Contributions By: Carol Carty
Illustrated By: QBN Studios

Quotes from the NIV Bible unless otherwise noted.

DEDICATION

This book is dedicated to my dear grandchildren and the Lord who blessed me with them.

***

My hope and prayer for all children is that the truths here will create many good discussions, and encourage turning to the Bible and the Lord for the answers.

Farm
Church
Beach
Pizza
Restaurant

Hello, Girls and Boys,

Let's read about some toys!

But first, let's join Noah and Noel to see where they will travel.

They are planning their trips, about to step onto the path of gravel!

As we follow along with them, we will learn some lessons about God.

He is like a shepherd guide who uses a sheep staff or rod!

When Noah and Noel visit a farm they see a kitten there.

The kitten seemed lost, he was running everywhere!

Noel decided to get the kitten, and give him a loving home.

To take care of little “Wally,” so he would never feel alone.

All of us are like Wally, we have a need to be found.

God comes to look for us, to give us His love without bound!

"For the Son of Man came to seek and to save the lost."
Luke 19:10

Noah and Noel are now playing on the beach, where they find small pebbles and stones.

They come in all shapes and sizes, but each is beautiful on its own.

The stones once looked rough and dirty, before the waves tossed them about.

They rolled and tumbled in the sea, now they're all smoothed out!

"...The crooked roads shall become straight, the rough ways smooth."

Luke 3:5

Life can make us feel the same, as those stones bumped and tossed around.

Hard times can seem so difficult, but with God we can calm down.

God works on us every day, to make us smooth and right.

Like the pebbles and stones on the beach, we become precious in His sight!

On Sundays, Noah and Noel attend a Church that is made of brick and mortar, different parts yet all held together.

That is so the Church building will last, through all kinds of stormy weather.

Another Church is all of us, who belong to God our Lord.

He holds us close like the mortar does, so we can be of one accord.

“neither height nor depth, nor anything else in all creation, will be able to separate us from the love of God...”

Romans 8:39

While buildings may not always last for many, many years,

God's Church which is made of you and me is stronger, so have no fears.

God's love will keep us close, and His Church will last forever.

We will never, ever be apart, for His promises you cannot sever!

After Church, Noah and Noel go with their friends to get pizza pies.

Each pizza slice has the same basic ingredients, but each is different in its size.

Some pieces are big and some are small, but each is part of a pie.

We call them each a treat, when they look so tasty to the eye!

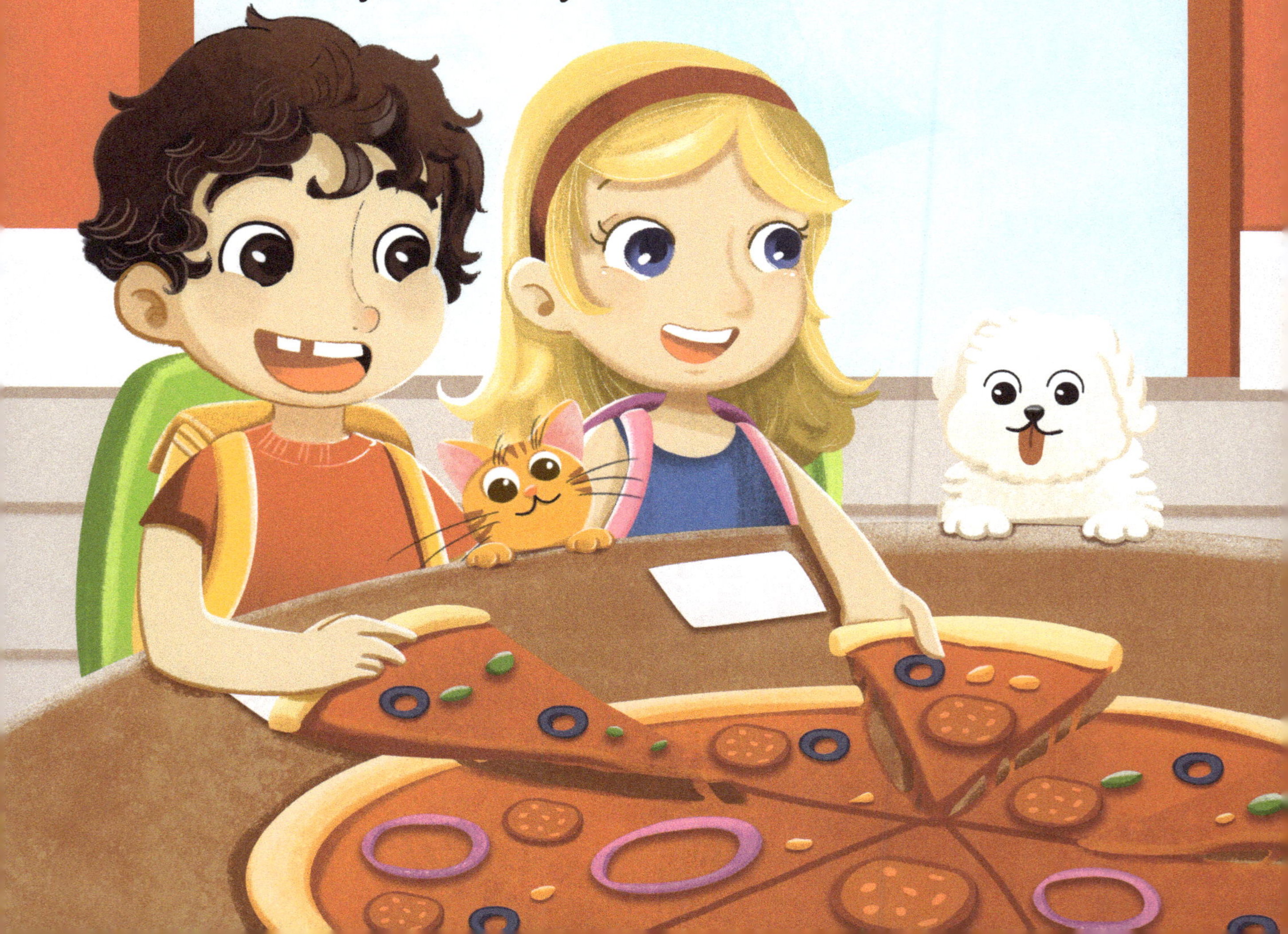

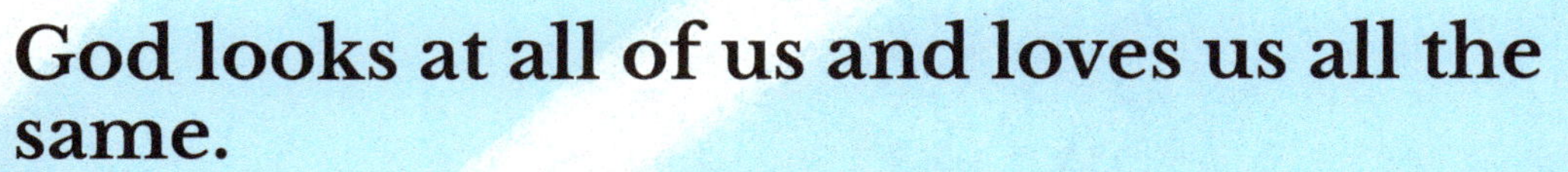

God looks at all of us and loves us all the same.

Whether we are very big or small, we are all children in His Holy Name!

“‘I now realize how true it is that God does not show favoritism.’”

Acts 10:34

After Church and getting pizza, Noah and Noel return to their houses and play with their toys.

Some toys are quiet, and some make noise!

Noel wants to make a model airplane, made from a kit full of parts.

The most important thing is the plan she needs to read from the start.

Once she puts it all together, she needs a rubber band.

This is used to create the power, which she'll wind up with her hand.

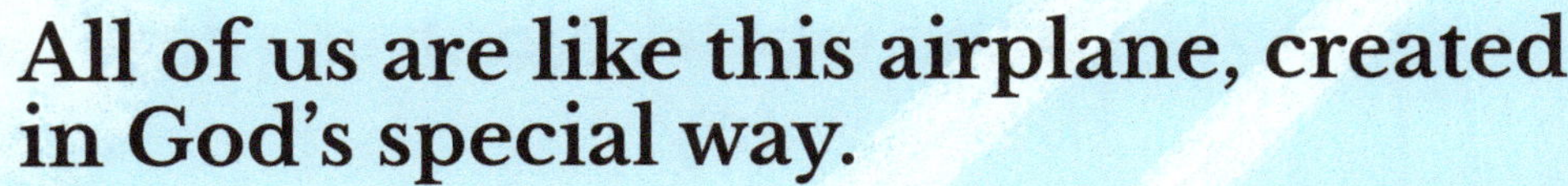

All of us are like this airplane, created in God's special way.

He has the perfect plan for us, and His Spirit powers us through the day!

"...being strengthened with all power according to his glorious might so that you may have great endurance and patience."

Colossians 1:11

Meanwhile, Noah is playing with his new toy,

Which brings him lots of joy!

The gyroscope was meant to move, it spins upon its axis.

Ships use them for stability, so they won't roll and break any glasses!

Spaceships, planes, and submarines, use many gyroscopes to guide.

They also help to steer and direct, which makes for a very smooth ride.

God wants us to move around, to tell others about His grace.

He will always keep us stable, and be our guide in any place!

"Lord, you give me stability and prosperity; you make my future secure."

Psalm 16:5 [NET]

Noah also enjoys playing his bugle, which you probably have heard.

It is often played at summer camp, it can create quite a stir!

They play it in the army to make soldiers fall in line.

Soldiers have to march around a lot, and learn to step “in time.”

We are in God's army, and His bugle is His Word.

It tells us which way to turn, so listen closely, undisturbed!

"Again, if the trumpet does not sound a clear call, who will get ready for battle?"

1 Corinthians 14:8

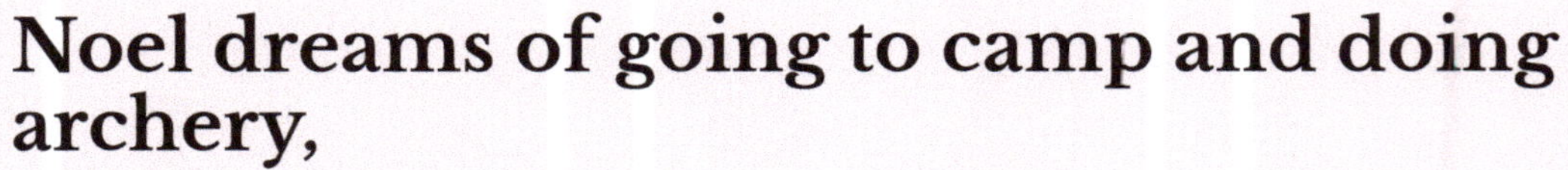

Noel dreams of going to camp and doing archery,

Using a bow and arrow to shoot, almost as far as she can see!

When she tries to shoot an arrow, she aims at the yellow bulls-eye,

It is at the center of the target, so she must focus and not shoot too high.

God wants us to be like arrows, that go straight toward His Son.

When we miss the special target, we can hurt more than one.

So press on towards this goal, try to read and pray a lot.

God will keep us going straight, to win His prize on the spot!

"Let your eyes look straight ahead; fix your gaze directly before you."

Proverbs 4:25

I hope you have enjoyed reading about Noah and Noel's trips and toys.

And may God bless you all, precious little girls and boys!

Remember that God is always with you, in all your ups and downs.

He knows when you are happy, and when you wear a frown!

He promises to stay near, wherever you may go.

He is your friend forever, and loves you more than you could ever know!

LESSON SUMMARIES AND ADDITIONAL VERSES

Adventures

LOST AND FOUND: Seek God

"... you will find him if you seek him with all your heart and with all your soul."

Deuteronomy 4:29

THE BEACH: God tries to improve you

"I will go before you and make the rough places smooth."

Isaiah 45:2a [NAS]

TO CHURCH: One with God

"Just as a body, though one, has many parts, but all its many parts form one body, so it is with Christ."

1 Corinthians 12:12

EATING TOGETHER: We are all children of God even though we look different

"...for you are all one in Christ Jesus."

Galatians 3:28

Toys

AIRPLANE: God has a plan for us, and His spirit gives us power

"But the plans of the Lord stand firm forever, the purposes of his heart through all generations."

Psalm 33:11

GYROSCOPE: We are to tell the world about Him, but we are unstable and need God to guide us

"He said to them, 'Go into all the world and preach the gospel to all creation.'"

Mark 16:15

BUGLE: God's bugle is the Bible

"The Lord thunders at the head of his army; his forces are beyond number, and mighty is the army that obeys his command."

Joel 2:11

BOW AND ARROW: Focus on God

"I press on toward the goal to win the prize for which God has called me heavenward in Christ Jesus."

Philippians 3:14

Acknowledgments

The author wishes to thank her daughter, Carol, for making this book a reality.

***

"To Him be the glory forever. Amen." Romans 11:36

About the Author

Nancy K. Carty's greatest joy is being a mother to three and a grandmother to six. She raised her children as a stay at home mom; was the local Brownie and Cub Scout troop leader; and the constant class volunteer mom. In her spare time, she was actively involved in the community as a volunteer for several non-profit organizations.

She is excited to see what the future holds for her!

Lightning Source UK Ltd.
Milton Keynes UK
UKHW050615111122
411979UK00003B/80

9 798987 018200